Chief Tony Umeh (Ochiri I)
& family~
Thank you for
your support!

God bless!

Content  Warning

To My Beloved Readers,

Please be advised, some of the poetry in this book touches upon difficult
and very sensitive topics, such as, abuse, child abuse, pedophilia, self-injurious
behavior, loss of a loved one, Obsessive-Compulsive Disorder (OCD),
racism, and slavery. Mature content. Discretion is advised.

I wish you well.

Love and blessings,

Pamela C. Nwokeji

First edition

Book design by Pamela C. Nwokeji

ISBN 978-1-7379343-0-1 (paperback)
ISBN 978-1-7379343-1-8 (ebook)
ISBN 978-1-7379343-2-5 (hardcover)

https://pamelacnwokeji.com/

Lilac Bush

A Poetic Journey and
Cultural Awakening for Future
Generations

Pamela C. Nwokeji

Dedicated to my grandma,

Doris Elizabeth Jones,

who is the

Inspiration for my creativity.

My angel.

Table of Contents

On Breakthrough

Acknowledgments

Bibliography

List of Figures

Preface

My name is Pamela C. Nwokeji (Bryant). I was born and raised in Boston, Massachusetts. I have an adoring, loving, strong mother who selflessly poured all of her love into my brother and me without the contribution of our biological father. My father abruptly abandoned us when I was two years old. We had no contact with him until I found him on my own in my mid-twenties. Since then, not much has come from our meeting. He hasn't given our relationship an honest try as a father or grandfather. But recently, on my last birthday, I received a call from him. It was the first time I'd ever heard his voice on my birthday. Unfortunately, and sadly, I am embarrassed to admit that I was incredibly happy. But I had to keep this excitement to myself because I thought it sounded ridiculous and shameful. A fifty-something-year-old woman longing for the moment she hears her estranged father wishing her a happy birthday for the first time sounds pathetic. But my feelings are human and, as stated, unfortunate because, obviously, I still desired for my father to acknowledge my existence.

I tell this story of my father because it is not uncommon among Black Americans today. Our expectations for Black American men, women, and families have diminished over the years, and this type of behavior from Black American fathers has become accepted as the norm. It has become our culture. During my life, I have worked hard to break this stigma of fatherlessness and the deteriorating parts of Black American culture I have been born into. I am motived and determined to end this cycle, and not pass it on to the next generation.

Currently, by the grace of God and a lot of hard work, I am doing very well in my life. I have a Bachelor's degree from Salem State University and a Master's Certification in Database Technology from the University of Massachusetts (Boston). I am Microsoft Certified and work as a Data Engineer. Also, I have an amazing husband and, together, we have four adult children who are doing

very well. My husband and I have made it a point to instill high goals and moral standards into our children to value themselves, their own families, education, and careers.

Realistically, I cannot do anything about my past. But I wrote this book because it's been therapeutic for me and, hopefully, it will be therapeutic for others. This book reflects on experiences in my life, in my family's lives, and people I've encountered throughout my life. My hope is this reflection will invoke thought and prompt self-reflection in the lives of others. I turn to the Black American community to connect with commonalities and ask pertinent questions. Not necessarily to get answers, but to ignite a movement of awareness, change, and improvement amongst each other. In a few areas of this book, I appeal to the Black American community to ask why we've normalized certain types of behavior adopted as culture.

In my opinion, it is necessary to speak words that seem to be taboo to us because we are in denial. Denial and blame-shaming others is not helping our people. We need to take ownership of the quality of life we choose to live to heal and grow. Otherwise, our problems will remain cyclical and continue to permeate our children's lives for generations to come.

Finally, writing poetry and digital drawing is a newfound love and talent. I figured, why not share it instead of pondering alone in thought?

Lift Ev'ry Voice and Sing[5] [6]

By James Weldon Johnson & J. Rosamond Johnson (1900)

Lift ev'ry voice and sing,
Till earth and heaven ring,
Ring with the harmonies of liberty;
Let our rejoicing rise,
High as the list'ning skies,
Let it resound loud as the rolling sea.
Sing a song full of the faith that the dark past has taught us,
Sing a song full of the hope that the present has brought us;
Facing the rising sun of our new day begun,
Let us march on till victory is won.

Stony the road we trod,
Bitter the chastening rod,
Felt in the days when hope unborn had died;
Yet with a steady beat,
Have not our weary feet,
Come to the place for which our fathers sighed?
We have come over a way that with tears has been watered,
We have come, treading our path through the blood of the slaughtered;
Out from the gloomy past,
Till now we stand at last
Where the white gleam of our bright star is cast.

God of our weary years,
God of our silent tears,
Thou who hast brought us thus far on the way;
Thou who hast by Thy might,
Led us into the light,
Keep us forever in the path, we pray.
Lest our feet stray from the places, our God, where we met Thee.
Lest our hearts, drunk with the wine of the world, we forget Thee.
Shadowed beneath Thy hand,
May we forever stand,
True to our God,
True to our native land.

Introduction

Every morning in elementary school, we would either pray or sing "Lift Ev'ry Voice and Sing," written and arranged by Civil Rights Activists, James Weldon Johnson and J. Rosamond Johnson, in the early 1900s. Whenever I heard this song growing up, it was always impassioned. With every word of the lyrics sung by so many of us throughout history, we connect with our ancestors. It brings to light the pain and exhaustion our ancestors have gone through in their quest and ultimate attainment of freedom. By singing this song, we, as Black Americans, lift our voice as free people. We celebrate our freedom in the place of all our African ancestors tortured and enslaved, those who lost their lives bound by slavery and never had the opportunity to be liberated. We celebrate for them and with them in song.

Black Americans have historically endured a great deal of pain and humiliation throughout the years. By today's standards, these humiliations would be inhumane. Yet, our ancestors survived these degradations, such as rape of our women while husbands helplessly watched, shackles, festering wounds, hangings, dogs devouring our flesh, unlawful killings, capital punishment, incarcerations, and much more. This abuse was all done at the hands of slave masters and our enemies. These experiences have left us broken, shattered, lost, and scattered. I often wonder what our African American ancestors, who bore the pains of our freedom, would say if they were alive today. They helplessly and involuntarily suffered through blood, sweat, and tears in hopes of and awaiting the freedom we have today. And now, officially, through our President Joe Biden, the 46th President of the United States of America, June 19th (Juneteenth), which acknowledges the abolishment of slavery, was officially made a federal holiday. As African Americans, we cannot take our freedom for granted. We must climb to the mountain top to appreciate our ancestors who went through this suffering and torture. Of course, our ancestors would be so proud and ecstatic about the achievements of so many of our honorable Black American inventors and leaders over time, such as: Madam CJ Walker, George Washington Carver, Martin

Luther King, Jr., Oprah, Patricia Bath, and so many more. And, also, they would be astounded and exhilarated by the first African American President, Barack Obama and the first African/Asian American Female Vice-President, Kamala Harris.

In our current Black American societal state, there is no one to blame but ourselves for many of the pains we are experiencing. The root cause of our current societal state is very relevant and acknowledged (as reflected upon in this text). But, can we veer away from leaning on our past pains to address our pitfalls, set higher goals, and achieve them? Let's take ownership of some of these issues and pull ourselves up and out to grow together. As of 2019, 64% of Black American children are raised in single-family homes[1], the highest of all other American races. Statistically, children raised by one parent: grow up with low self-esteem; have problems in school; are more likely to become involved in crime (including Black-on-Black senseless killings); at a greater risk of being abused by their mother's boyfriend or strangers; more likely to become single parents themselves with unknown fathers; and, less likely to graduate high school or attend college[2] which leads them to the welfare system resulting in cyclical poverty. Cyclical poverty exists across all races, but the Black American race stands as one of the highest in poverty among all American races[3]. If we care about our children's progress for generations to come, we will stop denying these worsening issues. We will stop making pacifying excuses. And we will move forward toward change and healing. As a Black American society, we have the power within ourselves and together to change course, improve, and pull ourselves out from these drawbacks. Our children deserve better.

Through my poetry, I celebrate many wonderful people and experiences. Also, I share some unfortunate incidents which occurred in my life and the lives of close family members in hopes that these experiences will be a catalyst for change and heightened awareness. I cannot change my past, but sharing these experiences may change someone's future for the better. Also, this book voices many of my concerns regarding the state of Black America today, including a

deteriorating, degrading culture such as fatherlessness, pants sagging, sexual promiscuity, Nigga calling, self-degradation, misuse of welfare, and the harmful, pernicious effects of abusive and misogynistic rap lyrics.

I also address police brutality and offenses against Black Americans by corrupt officers of the law. And to clarify, all officers of the law are not corrupt. We have many good, upstanding, honorable officers out there who serve with dignity to uphold the law. I have many in my family. However, there are a few corrupt, bad apples that need to be exposed.

Many of the issues I address in my book are general societal concerns such as fatherlessness. But, although it does exist everywhere, it is more prevalent among Black people. Other general concerns I specifically address are predators and molestation, to provide parents with awareness of the profile of predators so they can armor up to protect their children. In the U.S., sexual abuse occurs in 1 in 5 girls and 1 in 20 boys, and the abuser is almost always someone the family knows[4]. I also touch upon substance abuse as a general societal concern in my poetry.

In this book, I encourage progress, hard work, competitiveness, and success in all fields of profession here in the United States and throughout the world. Education is the key to pull ourselves up and out of poverty and into higher, more lucrative careers. My poetry speaks about healing, motivation, and higher learning. I advocate for parents to support their children and guide them through better education and, therefore, a better future. I also urge fathers to take a more significant role in their children's lives, no matter the circumstance. It is imperative and crucial for Black American fathers to be home or have 100% loyal relationships with their children.

Finally, and most importantly, these poems guide the reader through my spiritual journey to share the wonderments of God and the power and love He provides in daily life to give us courage and strength.

Risen to this place I stand now;

High above perceived expectations of me.

Molded into an image only God could endow;

His hands still forming for all to see.

Pamela C. Nwokeji, 2021

Lilac Bush

Free

Earth trembling beneath my feet,
In awe of the words spoken to me.
"You loved him!"
Rendered speechless as truth was
told.
In infancy, I loved you.
Now, in from the cold.

Alone so many years
On an island of shame.
Left as a bastard;
Where were you, man?
Now, I understand my frustration
and tears;
The anguish of inner turmoil for
so many years.

She shouted from within,
"Here he is!"
While covering abandonment pain.
In hopes that I would grasp,
But all was in vain.
Instead, dissatisfaction persistently
ensued;
Feeling cheated, always feeling
cheated, with faux you.

Advanced beyond my years,
Always questioning why.
The frustration of being lied to;
"Why won't he try?"

The proxy received the brunt of
my pain.
A connection so deep,
Thoughts innately ingrained.
A connection so deep,
Thoughts no one could erase.
A connection so deep,
No one could replace.

So, with reckless abandon
And void of all understanding;
With no key to hold
Or concrete landing;
I grasp on to what remains
And say let's try;
Hyper-focused and determined
Not knowing the reasons why.

I release inhibitions and clenches
of pain.
Let go the weight of disconnect,
distrust, and disdain.
Exhaustingly, trudging through
life's journey of loving me;
I can say, finally say, I feel free.

2 Lilac Bush

Figure 1: Free

Lilac Bush 3

On Children...

Children are our reward. They are a gift from
God.

Inspired by Psalm 127:3

Figure 2: A Secret

A Secret

A secret, when we were children, you asked me to keep;
Which, to my surprise, turned out no easy feat.
Standing in my room, we were hardly pubescent;
Desperation in your eyes for someone to listen.

You closed the door behind you for no one to hear.
The man your mom just married was touching you there.
Adrenaline took off. My heart began to race.
You read my reaction, the look on my face.

Such a huge amount of burden for a child to bear.
Your innocence was stolen, but you swallowed your fears.
Evil all around, but you chose to withstand;
Self-sacrifice for happiness, due to chaos unplanned.

You were born to be free; to go outside and play;
Enjoy the slides and swings on a beautiful day.
A promise of hope, with a future untold;
But, your light dimmed because a predator took hold.

My love for you, so strong; I'm happy you shared
Something so personal. Your heart to me bared.
Honored to know a hero so courageous and bold;
But with fear and trepidation, for your safety, I told.

Beth

A mental rollercoaster, Beth is forced to ride.
Her mom's ups and downs she begs to subside.
By the window, she awaits rescue from God.
Her things in a suitcase, it's gotten so hard.

The fast life with mom, she knows it so well.
With kids in the coatroom, Beth's thrown in to dwell.
While adults sang, laughed, and partied all night,
Sometimes these parties would end with a fight.

Her mom was addicted to laughter with friends.
Beth had so much fun; she didn't want it to end.
Because when they got home, transition began.
The cyclone of emotions all over again.

Her life is compared to being spun on a web.
Her mom constantly played games with her head.
Slowly, she sucked the blood from Beth's veins.
Challenging, for a child alone to sustain.

The rules mom established, Beth followed, so strict.
All things in their place; lined up perfect.
Items on the dresser were arranged in specific order.
Mom's OCD took the path to be a hoarder.

I witnessed how unfair Beth was treated.
When mom came home from partying, she'd get beaten.
A wrinkle in the bed while trying to sleep,
Caused Beth to take cover from a pounding so deep.

Sporadically, random items would fly.
A target, Beth pondered, questioning why.

Unpredictable, mom's mood, she wanted it to end.
Relief would drain when she pushed pins in her skin.

She's thinking: Where's God? Will He come to my rescue?
Praying He saw all she was going through.
But God in His infinite wisdom and love
Saw all Beth went through from Heaven above.

Through thick and thin, He's always been there
With love and strength to sustain and bear.
Over and over, He's left the ninety-nine.
Under His wings, Beth, you will find.

Figure 3: Beth

Monster in the Playroom

There's a monster in the
playroom
With legs open wide.
A monster in the playroom;
He wants me to ride.

The game he created,
Was run-round and fall
On him writhing in pleasure.
"Should parents we call?"

A monster in the playroom;
He called it a game.
A monster in the playroom;
Things were never the same.

With each fall discomfort,
On the floor between his legs.
With each fall, breath constricted,
"Please stop," to him, I begged.

A monster in the playroom;
Small kids all around.
He was entrusted by the parent.
He told us not to make a sound.

Found courage to break away;
"I'm telling," I said.
Desperately down the hallway,
Brother in hand, I led.

"Quick! Hurry! The man!"
I said with shy urgency.
"He's doing something wrong,"
But she said she had company.

Facing him again,
Sweating, "What did she say?"
She didn't believe me
But my mom, she may.

To my house, we ran quickly.
Convinced, my mom wanted to
hear.
"The man, he did something!"
But another deaf ear.

A monster in the playroom;
The truth was exposed.
A monster in the playroom;
Now secrets they hold.

Pointing and whispering
With nothing addressed.
Knew something wrong
happened;
But left to guess.

"He's a monster," the grands said.
I still didn't understand.
A monster in the playroom?
But he looked like a man.

10 Lilac Bush

Figure 4: Monster in the Playroom   Lilac Bush 11

Figure 5: Diamond in the Rough

Diamond in the Rough

You were an angel of beauty;
And placed here unscathed.
You were a diamond that
sparkled;
And, awestruck, we gazed.

You were a prodigy in our
presence.
"Has she been here before?"
Your fragility was like an egg
To protect from vultures.

But, in swooped that vulture
With his talons held tight.
Our gift by God was stolen
As we slept in the night.

Talons were released
And you were dropped at our
feet.
You were tattered and stained.
Your scars, painfully ingrained.

Those incessant thoughts pecking;
Those bad memories untold.
You were violated and abused,
But you handled it so bold.

Your suffering was not in vain.
Now at peace in Heaven above.
No bad memories or pain;
In our hearts, forever loved.

You were here for a season
And God said enough.
You will never be forgotten.
A Diamond in the Rough.

Lilac Bush 13

A Reason

Were you in prison? Is that why, after years, you appear?
If so, there's no judgment. Please talk, I can hear.
Were you a marine on active duty and stuck out at sea?
A secret agent undercover, concealed life, you had to flee?

In a desert for many years, in a POW camp?
If this were the case, you're a hero and a champ.
Hmm? An injury to your head would have given you amnesia!
Did you lose your way and somehow end up in Tunisia?

Or maybe as time passed, you didn't know how to break
through;
A connection lost, uncomfortable, appearing out of the blue.
In that case, did you watch me on my way to school?
Or, on summer days, did you watch me have fun at the pool?

Did you think I'd be better off because you had no money?
Did you think I would not love you because your days were not
so sunny?
Did you think I could handle it because your father left you?
Or you blamed it on my mother because she was no longer
your boo?

Love knows no limits, has no boundaries or lines.
Love is endless with no space and no time.
Love ignores weather. It's better on rainy days.
Love breaks down barriers in so many ways.

Just one explanation would be simple and fair;
Accepted no matter what, because I'll know that you care.
Clarification would shed light and be a sacrifice for us;
The first step on our journey of new love and trust.

Figure 6: A Reason

Figure 7: Angel Borrowed

Angel Borrowed

But when your child from God is staring in your face;
Borrowed from Heaven; from the throne of grace;
Assigned to love and cherish in this time and space;
In this presence of greatness, you bring disgrace.

We are lower than the angels. This child should be praised.
An angel assigned by God. You should be amazed.
To protect and guide is serious and not a phase.
Royal visitor to you entrusted, an honor to raise.

As in curling, two sweep and make the path clean;
For that rock to glide on a course they make gleam.
You should do the same for your king or queen.
Intensely sweep their way clear and make pristine.

A test by God, you're appointed as a royal escort;
To protect from the enemy; keep them safe and secure;
To love, hold high, reassure and nurture;
Until well-rounded, educated, respectful and mature.

"Train up a child in the way he should go."
God saw you and a perfect match He bestowed;
To love, honor, cherish, protect and hold;
This angel on earth from God borrowed.

Figure 8: Believe Fuel

Believe Fuel

With your belief beneath his wings,
Your child can do anything.
He can thrust to the stars
Like a rocket ship so far.

Shooting up to the sky,
With wings, he can fly
Like a bird or a plane
Or even Superman.

If you believe in your son,
With achievements, he'll stun.
Just instill high goals
And, with your direction, he'll go

To places you've never been.
He'll win victories unseen.
Your confidence is his throttle.
Your vision is his model.

Just fuel him with "Believe."
You'll be amazed at what he'll achieve.

Be careful of how you treat your children.

Their angels always await instructions from

God.

Inspired by Matthew 18:10

22 Lilac Bush

Figure 9: Secret Place

Secret Place

That raging evil, with fire in her
Eyes,
Came into your bedroom tonight,
Again.

And with the strength of an angry
Man, laughing and screaming,
You are the object of her hand and
The reason for her pain.

You take blows into the bed with
Rhythmic pounds.
Your name resounds as I feel the
Bed bounce up and down.

And you take cover in a fetal
Position, receiving this fury from
Hell.

In your eyes, I see someone
Undeserving of this.

I see love.
I see beauty.
I see freedom.

So, with imagination, we drift.

First, our fingers as earplugs until
We hear the ringing sound;

Then we are released with hugs
Into a burst of freedom!

Now, in this place, where you
Belong, full of wonder and joy,
We are surrounded by welcoming
Songs.

Dancing in beautiful swirling
Colors,
We are ballerinas twirling to music
On stage.

An audience looks on with a
Starstruck gaze,
And they love you. They're all
Amazed

At your magic,
Your grace,
Your pureness,

......So pretty,

Your talent,
Joy,
Laughter, and humor,

......So witty.

They see what I see.

So, we stay here until it ends.

Lilac Bush 23

24 Lilac Bush

Figure 10: Grandma's Art Dresser

Grandma's Art Dresser

Grandma was an artist.
She had a dresser filled with
supplies.
As children, going through it,
We couldn't believe our eyes.

Under her direction,
We made creative art.
We had so much fun
Exploring desires of our hearts.

For some, her art dresser
Resembled a big mess.
But the world it meant to her,
And to us, it was the best.

With paints on canvas and paper,
Landscapes came alive.
Rivers with bodies of water,
So real, we wanted to dive.

With clay and a spinning wheel,
We would mold and make watery,
Mounds of clay we could feel
And shape great pottery.

African masks were formed
With plaster molds from our faces.
Tribal colors adorned,
Took us to cultural places.

Pastel-colored tissue paper
Used with long green wires;
And brush handles used as shapers
Made bouquets of flowers
admired.

Grandma's art dresser;
A chaotic disarray of colors;
Bonded us together
And brought beauty and joy to
others.

Predator

Manipulatively deceptive,
He is always around.
Disabling all defenses,
A thief with no sound.

Parents conned stupid;
They think he's their friend.
Innocence he steals,
While camouflaged, he blends.

Courting and buying,
Constantly trying,
Always available,
So helpful and stable,

Touch here, glimpse there,
Over a long while;
Slight rub on the back,
All done with a smile.

A hand on the knee,
A touch with caress;
Oh, why can't you see
His hand up her dress?

Opportunities he creates
As he lies in wait.
He snapped a few twigs.
If listening, you'd wake.

Gem in your possession,
He tarnished, he stained.
All done while you were looking;
Destruction and ruins remain.

A stranger came in.
He preyed on the weak.
Weak parents and victim;
Now solace you seek.

"A wolf in sheep's clothing?"
"Why didn't she scream?"
From babe, tight holding,
In her eyes, trust gleams.

A monster in satire,
A devil, a sleaze;
"Set him on fire!"
"Bring him to his knees!"

"Torture and jail him!"
"He introduced her to sin!"
"He's a scumbag, a creep, a liar!"
But you let a predator in.

26 Lilac Bush

Figure 11: Predator

28 Lilac Bush   Figure 11: Through a Child's Eyes

Through a Child's Eyes

Sitting in my chair, just over the age of one;
Mom was watching the news that night.

Behind me, she was crying and distraught;
As scenes flashed in black and white.

She said, "Pam, don't ever forget this day."
A Black man was down; people were pointing in shock.

That was the day our lives forever changed;
The day Martin Luther King Jr. was shot.

30 Lilac Bush

Figure 13: Debbie

Debbie

Throughout the neighborhood, her laughter bellowed so loud.
After school, grandma said, my mom always drew a crowd.
Playing jump rope with a bra she grew out of too quick,
Was loved by the boys because she was well-endowed.

Skin so dark and sweet, like milk chocolate;
Voice so deep and smooth, like velvet;
Hair pressed and curled with curvy stature;
She could get any boy, have him right in her pocket.

Her conversations always filled with joy and laughter.
So much fun with her, breath you'll try to capture.
Her signature laugh, ha-ha-ha-haaa, so funny, you'll cry.
Sit back and relax. You may need a nap after.

My grandma said she could make friends with a fly.
Friends to laugh and cry,
Friends to sing, dance and buy,
Friends to share and confide,
Friends up to the sky.

In her carefree spirit, they all long to bide.
Knowing Debbie's like taking a joyful ride,
With friends, hands thrown up to your favorite song loud.
"That Debbie," my grandma said. "She always drew a crowd."

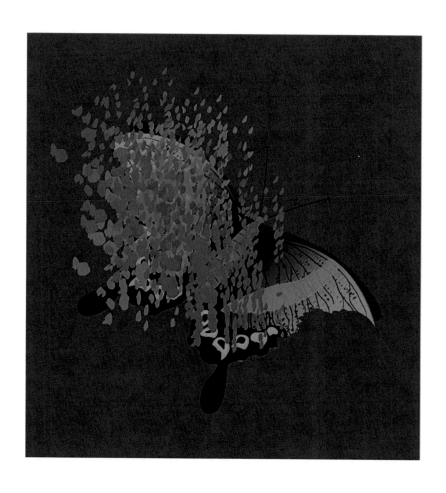

Figure 14: Butterfly Fly

Butterfly Fly

Her magnificence is covered with dust.
Ruined by environmental lust.
Fluttering in ashes and dirt,
This butterfly, her wing is hurt.

Injured, she knows she can't stay.
Tired in her fight to fly away.
Brilliant colors, they can't see;
Stifled by their careless debris.

Be devoted and honor your child above yourself.

Inspired by Romans 12:10

Her King

He doesn't notice the roughness of her skin
As he holds her hand walking to school.
Grinning, burying her struggle within;
Working third shift can be so cruel.

Dad disappeared before he turned one
Leaving mom to figure things out.
So, she selflessly pours all her love in their son,
While his dad took the easy way out.

He doesn't inquire about where his dad is;
He just basks in the love his mom gives.
Every morning, she greets him with a kiss.
The sacrifice is tough, but for his life, she lives.

Day in and day out, mom's schedule is demanding;
From housework to shift work at night.
Washing dishes, mopping floors, and handling
So many chores make staying awake a fight.

Her representation of mom and dad
Is difficult, but pleasure it brings.
All worth it through good times and bad,
Because she's molding and raising her king.

Figure 15: Her King

Figure 16: Their Fight

Their Fight

Your child's fight is not always what it seems.
They're fighting for their dignity,
Which outsiders perceive to be rebellion and indignity.
This fight says, I need your love and protection.
This fight says, YOU need hope and redemption.
That cesspool you've dragged them in;
That mess you chose to begin;
They're in it with no way out.
They're in it without a doubt.
Please bring their misery to an end
And come to terms with some conviction.
Make right of the wrongs you've created.
Stop blaming them for being jaded.
What they're in is what you've made it.

40 Lilac Bush

Figure 17: Bastard Blend

Bastard Blend

Bastard upon bastard;
With all our bastard friends.
Trusting in paths broken,
Pain carried within.

Strength found in our bonding.
We are naive and content.
Challenges faced daily,
But together, "Don't we blend?!"

Not Your Time

Boxes full of salamanders,
A pocket full of frogs,
Trudging through grass and dirt,
To capture worms under logs.

Mud pies wound up on your tongue.
You enjoyed it when we screamed.
Jumping from the second-floor porch
Was not a clever scheme.

Adventure was your middle name;
Having fun with your small friends.
Running our street and playing games;
Always going until the day would end.

A winter coat with shorts,
One summer day you wore.
Hit and run by a drunk in transport,
Brakes screeched, and there you were.

You recalled your soul began to rise.
You saw me over you cry.
That day you touched the hand of God
But He said, "It's not your time."

Figure 18: Not Your Time

***Note: Illustration is parent walking child to school

44 Lilac Bush

Figure 19: Take Them to School

Take Them to School

One foot, you kicked out the door,
And then a hand, too.
Dragging on the cold ground
As the stranger grabbed you.

So young when he persuaded
You to get into the car.
Now fighting for your life,
You're halfway on the tar.

God saved you that morning,
Alone, while walking to the bus.
You fought like a lion
To get back home to us.

Rescued by an angel who saw
That struggle so cruel.
Brought you back home safely;
Because they should've walked you to school.

Since Five

She's been left alone in the darkness
And alienated since five;
Invalidated and confused;
Never seen as abused when compared.

Forced into a desolate place;
She felt the brunt of full disgrace
By a man her age times ten
Who tarnished her innocence.

But remained strong
When she was wronged;
And made her own happy face.

Buried deep in memory,
The feeling of his touch.
Haunting and never-ending.
Asphyxiation from tongue thrusts.

The scent of his cologne
Will never leave her.
The smell of his sweat
Will always grieve her.

The feeling of discomfort
When he touched her there;
While laughing, enjoying
And thriving off her fear.

Then telling and getting scolded
For wrongs she did not own.

Expectations remain too high;
For this secret, until she dies.

She's been tasked to bear
Secrets that made relatives
Stop, look and stare
As if she were an alien.

But never talked to
Or counseled;
Just left alone to survive.......

..........Since five.

Figure 20: Since Five

Love your children as God loves you.

Inspired by John 15:12

Black Girl in Hiding

Beautiful Black girl so bruised and battered,
Step out from your fortress of intimate shadow.
Built from the pain and disappointments of past,
This pain and darkness cannot always last.

Step out from hiding under overcasts of fear;
And your mesmerizing beauty, we promise not to stare.
You're a gorgeous being from God created;
A gorgeous being of God who is jaded.

So valuable and magnificent in color you are;
But you choose to cover and conceal due to scars.
Self-mutilate, self-abuse by appearing unattractive;
With words, deeds, clothing, and jewelry distractive.

We see you in hiding in your dungeon of shame.
No need for disguise; we love you the same.
Scars don't define you. They reveal your strengths.
Step out from the darkness and yourself you will thank.

Figure 21: Black Girl in Hiding

Dating a Pervert

His mind is not on how gorgeous you look,
How smart you are, or even how you cook;
Your curves, so attractive, and the way you walk;
So adorable, your lips appear when sexy you talk.

You wonder where he has been all your life.
You hope he'll propose and make you his wife.
He's so kind, even with the crap you output;
He's so perfect! Waits on you hand and foot.

Together, as a couple, you make an ideal pair.
He's a gentleman, so romantic, how in your eyes he stares.
The day you two met felt like nothing but fate.
But have you looked closely? He's nothing but a fake!

Open your eyes! If you clear them, you'll see.
He's actually a wolf wearing the clothing of sheep.
Have you wondered why he hovers and you can't breathe?
Alienation from your family is what he's achieved.

So cunning and misleading, he's weaseled his way in.
And to your children, he's been a "special" friend;
Playing "special" games when you're not home;
Romances them with "special" gifts when they're alone.

Horny in the night, your child's room, he sneaks in;
Violating your child's body as you are sleeping;
Touching in private spots that make them uncomfortable;
And swearing your baby to secrecy by feeding them bull****.

I know this is hard but, pay attention, my words are true.
You were never his focus. He's a pervert and never loved you.

52 Lilac Bush

Don't think twice! Listen! Get rid of him, please!
He's a criminal, conman, liar, and a sleaze!

So, don't wallow in self-pity and sit around wondering why.
When confronted with your child's truth, don't think it's a lie;
Or self-abuse, lie around, and endlessly cry;
Be a soldier! Kick him out, and don't say goodbye!

Focus on your children; counsel, huddle and heal.
Hover over them, be protective, and talk to them real.
Apologize! Tell them it's your fault, and then,
Be careful in the future, so this never happens again.

Figure 22: Dating a Pervert

Line Up

He's been pointed out in a lineup,
And you're sure it's not your child.
Raised him from birth to grownup;
This accusation is way too wild.

How in the world did it come to this?
This is completely insane.
Was it something that you missed?
You start to pick your brain.

In line behind the plexiglass,
He looks like all the rest.
Viewed by all as lower class
And not society's best.

Figure 23: Line Up

He's demeaned and degraded.
He stands in line exposed.
Exhaustingly interrogated;
You know how the story goes.

But give this further thought.
Reach deep into your mind.
Reject those lies you sold and bought.
If you seek, then you will find.

Why was there a gun in his car?
Have you thought about that?
If you think about it, not so bizarre,
They found drugs under his car mat!

Rewind again a little bit more
To that night he was out with friends.
Oh yeah, and why was he in that store?
Confused, you don't know where he's been!

Now giant steps back a couple years
To those friends he was hanging around.
Did you adamantly tell them to disappear?
Did you give heed to those warning sounds?

Did you hammer college into his head?
Or talk to him about his career?
Did you challenge him to think ahead?
Or for a better life, he's unaware?

Figure 24: Sister

Sister

In my room, on my bed,
With pillows, we all played.
You jumped off with laughter.
Our eyes on you stayed.

Disappointed you were leaving,
You looked back with delight.
We begged for a reason,
You said, "I'll stay the night."

With morning, a revelation,
Just a dream once again.
Brushed off as imagination
But a tug of doubt remained.

Our brother called that day.
With this, my life changed.
You passed away.
Then a multitude of emotions
ranged.

Due to our father's aloofness,
There was nothing between us.
Disconnect and distance,
Brought suspicion and distrust.

New images of your beauty
Surfaced pain from within.
A whole life passed before me.
How could this happen?

Tears flooded every morning
Upon opening my eyes.
Drops glided down my face;
Could not help but cry.

We never met in this life
Due to circumstances not right.
But in my dreams, you visited me
And stayed for one night.

Lilac Bush 57

On Neighborhood...

Love your neighbors.

Inspired by Mark 12:31

Kensington Street

Kensington, a street for the urban middle class.
During summers, every child gathered for games in mass.
We played on this street, having fun happily.
Laughter echoed through the air as we all felt carefree.

From neighboring streets, kids came to have fun.
A multitude of games, we played every one.
From hopscotch to jump rope, until nightfall;
Until we were exhausted; until our mothers called.

Kickball was one of our favorite games;
A two-team street sport with a competitive aim.
Kick the ball and run around to home base.
Sometimes you'd fall from a loose shoelace.

Jump rope and hopscotch were played by boys and girls.
With singles and double-dutch, we'd give the rope a twirl.
Singing while jumping until you were out;
You were a pro if you could jump and turnabout.

Our best game was probably hide-and-go-seek.
You'd always get caught from your spot when you peeked.
Or there was another game called "Not It,"
You ran from the "It" until you were hit.

Our moms didn't care how long we were out there;
Running around until dusty without a care.
Except when hungry, we'd take a lunch break and eat,
Or walk to the convenience store to buy junk food and sweets.

The best nights would end with a game called Rattlesnake.
Forming a line singing hand-to-hand, this line you could not break.

Looping under each connection until the very end,
Finally, we screamed "RATTLESNAKE!" while entangled with our
friends.

The best times in life are when you're young and carefree.
Summers on Kensington, from our homes, we would flee.
To gather together with good friends in our neighborhood.
Also, fresh air and exercise did us some good.

Figure 25: Kensington Street

Boulevard Wall

Sitting on this brick boulevard wall
On a hot summer day, and the wind is still.
My mom, from the porch, calls us to eat
Because she's cooking hot dogs on the grill.

Air fills with exhaust smoke and the ground
Reverberates with loud music from sports car races.
As teenage boys chase cute girls walking with oiled
Legs and creative sneaker laces.

Groups of kids, with rolled towels count their change
As they walk across this road to the pool.
Drunken Joe directs traffic while stumbling
And shouting profanities, like a fool.

On the courts, guys are sweating, laughing loudly
And playing basketball; their favorite sport.
Pivoting and ducking, arms flying and blocking,
Sneakers pound as they run back and forth.

Children stop what they're doing on the playground.
They even abandon their swings.
Pulling moms off their porches and running,
As the ice cream truck rolls by and sings.

The sound of mom's voice echoes louder this time.
We were hanging on this wall to chill.
Observed activities are many. From this wall,
There is plenty, although the wind is still.

Figure 26: Boulevard Wall

Lilac Bush 63

On Women...

To find a good woman is far more valuable than precious jewels.

Inspired by Proverbs 31:10

African Queen

Awestruck by her beauty, she is
Fascinating in her realm. Her love shines
Radiantly and can be felt with fiery,
Impassioned emotions. She intertwines
Confidence with purpose to achieve her goals.
Abundant are her efforts to succeed.
Naturally, she is gifted with profound resilience.
Quenched are thirsts privileged to drink from her well.
Unconditional love is what she has to offer;
Embodying all that is fierce and attractive;
Emboldened by love of family, friends and life;
Noble is the character of this African Queen!

Figure 27: African Queen

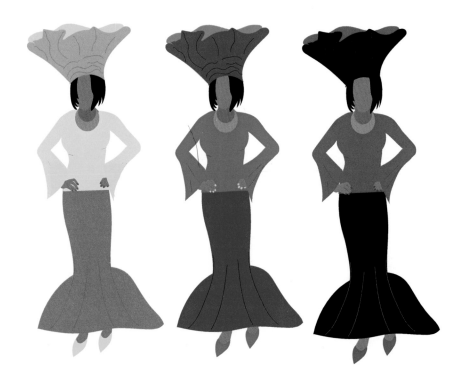

68 Lilac Bush

Figure 28: Field of Roses

Field of Roses

From deeply rich soil, this African Rose sprouts;
Glorifying God with beauty devout.
Her colors are abundant; the array is so rare;
No flower on earth could ever compare.

Up from red earth, her culture takes root;
From diamonds and oil, she rises and shoots.
Strong in her faith, in worship, she blooms.
Love for her family, she adoringly plumes.

Strength of her stem, which holds up her flower
Can weather a storm with unlimited power.
Her leaves wrap her children from harsh winds that blow.
Her thorns protect them when the enemy is too close.

Her love for her husband, so loyal and true,
With gratitude, she's kissed by the morning dew.
Dedication to family makes her toil and work hard.
She sacrifices so much, herself, she disregards.

Carefully clothed with each layer of petals;
She's adorned with bold patterns of vibrant apparel;
A queen deserving and crowned with her head tie
Wrapped uniquely with layers raised high.

When gathered together for cultural occasions,
With others in her likeness befitting her equation,
There is colorful dancing to a song she composes;
A vision of splendor, this Field of Roses!

Queendom Fatigue

As she enters her house,
She's cleaning while walking.
So many mom questions,
Confusion while talking.

Into her arms,
Her kids give big hugs.
So tight with excitement,
Bags fall to the rug.

Waiting on dinner,
Their stomachs are growling
Including her husband's;
He kisses his darling.

Like an octopus,
Her hands are cooking and cleaning.
Unpacking the food;
They're not good at housecleaning.

In no time, it's done.
The family is fed;
Next homework and attention;
Then the kids to bed.

A sigh of relief
And feeling quite ragged;
She crashes on the bed
Half sleep and tired.

In awe of her super powers,
He holds her like a glove.
She still has strength left
So she gives her man some love.

70 Lilac Bush

Figure 29: Queendom Fatigue

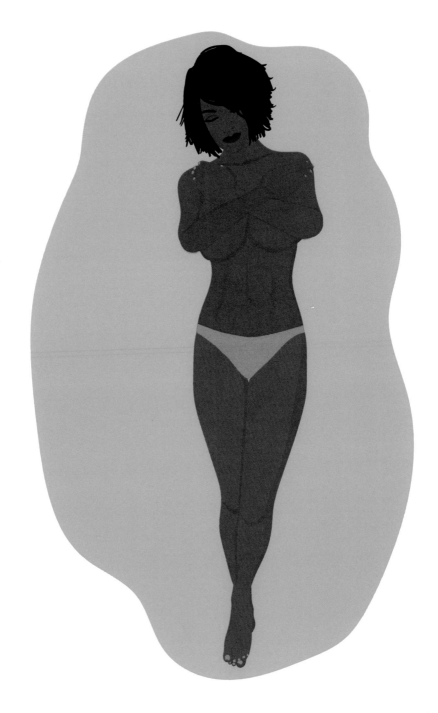

Figure 30: Cycle

Cycle

Hey, welcome back.
She's not glad to see your face again.

It's been a while, but it feels the same;
She takes one more, added, to blend.

That nauseating feeling, she feels, with no pride;
Stripped down to nakedness and nothing;

Now, here you are, back with that fake smile.
She forgives you, but this is so tiring.

Figure 31: Black Man, Do You See Her?

Black Man, Do You See Her?

Black man, do you see her?
She's standing in your view.
You are not invisible.
She actually sees you.

Black man, do you see her?
She makes your skin crawl.
She resembles the struggle.
That black hole you won't fall.

Black man, do you see her?
There is a disconnect.
You only see her flaws.
To you, she's imperfect.

Black man, do you see her?
She looks too much like you.
Are you so self-deprecating,
Those others you pursue?

Her love is passionate and bold;
Worth more than diamonds and
gold;
Profound love to take ahold;
Just waiting to enfold.

She's educated and well-raised.
Her love is not a phase.
To engage her, you'll be amazed;
A queen who awaits your gaze.

Swirled colors of chocolate dip;
Soft, sweet-tasting, full lips;
Curvaceous body to her hips;
Just waiting for your grip.

Black man, do you see her?

Lilac Bush 75

On Deadbeat Dads...

Any man who does not provide for his children
is a man who doesn't believe in God.

Inspired by 1 Timothy 5:8

Picture

There's a picture of a man
That always seems to fall
Out of the pages
Of her baby book.

It is that picture
She obsessively, throughout
The years, at times,
Goes to find.

It tumbles to the ground
Slowly in the air
With twists and turns;
But always saved
Before it touches the floor
With a desperation
She cannot explain.

Attempting to connect the
Importance of this photo
She caresses
Tightly in her hand,
With significance
She can no longer brand;

She just stares.

And tries to understand
Why it's years worn
And close to torn with
A creased face she can
No longer see.

Figure 32: Picture

Lilac Bush 79

When the Black Dad Isn't Home

When the Black dad isn't home,
In mind, body nor spirit,
She sits on the throne alone.
All onus, she must bear it.

His children suffer greatly;
When the Black dad isn't home.
Filling this void innately,
Causes them to roam.

Poverty, his kids are prone;
Lack of higher education.
When the Black dad isn't home,
Her direction is less taken.

His dwelling, an easy target;
Thieves and perverts come to comb;
Stealing his priceless assets;
When the Black dad isn't home.

When the Black dad isn't home,
In mind, body nor spirit,
Built strongholds are torn down
And their screams, he can't hear it.

Their journey becomes a maze;
When the Black dad isn't home.
Stumbling under a haze;
Their way confusing and unknown.

Inequalities are condoned
And disparities are stronger.
When the Black dad isn't home;
They assume he cares no longer.

Like a ship needs a captain
To navigate tides strong,
His family will have a greater mission
When the Black dad comes back home.

80 Lilac Bush

Figure 33: When the Black Dad Isn't Home   Lilac Bush 81

Cockroach

You hide like a cockroach
But soon light will appear
To expose you in your corner;
Then you'll scatter with fear.

In the darkness, you are concealed.
In the corner, you choose to hide.
Skeletons in your closet;
In your mind, they will subside.

I see you in your corner.
You've already been exposed.
Just choose not to take my shoe
And crush you to dispose.

So, go ahead and keep hiding;
Every corner, continue to flee.
Soon someone will come and squash you.
Someone better than me.

Figure 34: Cockroach

Black Dad

Turned your back on your
children;
Now you're raising someone
else's.
Squatting in a family built-in;
Don't you think that is selfish?

When you face your girlfriend's
offspring,
Do you see your own?
You hide like a weakling,
To say you have a home.

You take her kids to school;
Then pick them up at noon.
Denying your kids is cruel.
You look like a buffoon.

Do you say, "I don't know,"
When asked about your babies?
No desire to see them grow?
You're spineless and lazy.

Your children need you, fool!
Don't convince yourself
otherwise.
If you say everything's cool,
You're like the devil, creating lies.

Can you accept a man in your
place?
If so, you'll have regrets.
Every day they'll look in HIS face.
Step up! They won't forget.

Call them on a daily.
They need this in their lives.
And let them know you love
them.
Otherwise, they'll feel deprived.

Don't let welfare raise your kids.
The State is not their dad.
Dependence, you must forbid.
For this, they will be glad.

Your kids, they need a role model;
So don't go run and hide.
They desire to be held and
coddled.
C'mon man, where's your pride?!

So today, please be their hero.
Selfishness, you must defy.
Don't settle as a zero.
And please do a lot more than
"try."

84 Lilac Bush

Figure 35: Black Dad   Lilac Bush 85

Shell of a Man

So now she is pregnant; carrying a life inside;
Stripped of all dignity and stripped of all pride.
That thing who knocked her up is gone, disappeared.
Abandoned, and left her naked with fear.

If you think of it, he has never been there;
Just a shell of a man to check out and stare;
A shell of a man who is pleasant to the eyes;
A shell of a man whose handsomeness belies.

The first time they met, his looks drove her crazy.
His eyes were light brown, and one eye was lazy.
A six-pack, so tight, long lashes and bowlegs;
She dreamed of loving him in so many ways.

His hair matched his eyes with springy, tight curls.
His muscles defined and loved by the girls.
Popping, locking, and floating, he could surely dance.
He held her so tight; could definitely romance.

But although she thinks his looks are so cool,
He barely made it to graduate high school.
He lives with his mother and doesn't pay rent;
Doesn't have a job; can't give her one cent.

Knocked up by a shell of emptiness and nothing;
No respect or values to give her a ring or something;
No home, car, or money to raise this beautiful baby.
He's floating through life cute, lost, and lazy.

Are good looks and cute supposed to pay the bills?
Can he put food on the table for his family with grills?

Can he get a job with his popping and locking dance?
Or love her and be there through any circumstance?

A shell of a man who looks good on the outside;
But when that shell's cracked, empty on the inside.
A shell of a man with nothing to offer;
A shell of a man, when you see him, don't bother.

Figure 36: Shell of a Man   Lilac Bush 87

On Honorable Men...

Honorable, is the man who lives an upstanding life; his children will inherit his blessings.

Inspired by Proverbs 20:7

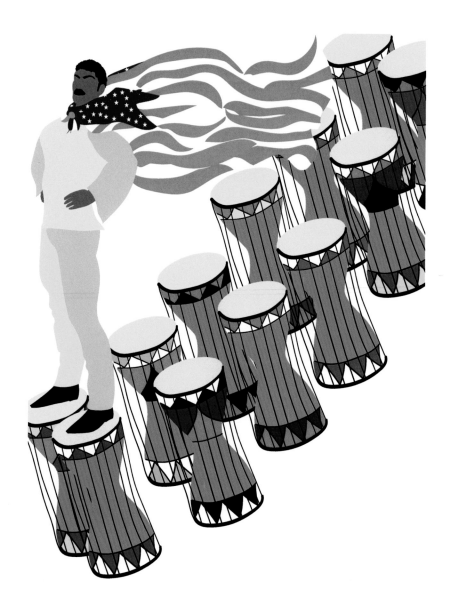

90 Lilac Bush

Figure 37: New African American

New African American

First-class seat to America, the African man arrives.
So, don't think you can break him or steal any pride.

On ancestors' shoulders, entitled and audacious;
His confidence is derived; bold, fearless, and courageous.

Footsteps like drumbeats pounding on lion skin;
Fearless of inequality, treading paths Black Americans never been.

Pronunciation of his name transports you to his village;
Unbroken succession passed down; to carry it is a privilege.

With education, he's in a career to look them in the eyes.
Stereotypes he dismantles, when encountered, they're surprised.

With the strength of a superhero, closed doors, he breaks through.
He's self-determined and eager; he relentlessly pursues.

Family means the world, his children, he conditions.
Imparts what he has learned and builds in them ambitions.

Knocking down all barriers, he builds his legacy.
Making his mark brazenly on new territory.

Final Salute

Methodically down the aisle,
Each slow step represents,
Your sacrifice for our country.
His elbows slightly bent.

One foot in front of the other;
Your casket at the end.
His eyes are sharply focused,
On a stranger but a friend.

With mechanical animation,
He draws nearer to you.
You're both fiercely connected
With love for the red, white, and blue.

With a salute, his hand is slanted.
His honor to stand beside.
Your final wish is granted.
With love for your country you died.

Figure 38: Final Salute   Lilac Bush 93

Figure 39: White Widow

White Widow

Patiently, in the center of this web she's weaved,
She waits for the prey she's worked hard to mislead.
She satisfies his needs before his thoughts are conceived.
He naively thinks she's got his back, but he's deceived.

Just going about his business thinking he has a friend;
But a friend cleverly unseeable, in waiting, she blends.
With each generous favor, she methodically descends
Upon him, as he sticks to this web she spins.

He's too busy to give a second thought to her clever scheme;
Too successful in his realm to figure out what this means.
Future goals of money, she's an opportunist and clings
To the meal ticket he holds, so her silk keeps wrapping.

Coffee before he wakes; there's a knock on the door.
Before one drop of rain, an umbrella, she has one more.
Cleans his car spotless; she handles his chores.
Incessantly present, before he realizes, he adores.

But love has nothing to do with this. He's blind to the con.
It may take years for him to see, in her game, he's a pawn.
In the meantime, she's good, and loves him from dusk to dawn.
But it's the bank account she's after, void of love and emotion.

Next, he's wrapped up tight while happy and defenseless;
An idiot who thought his friends' warnings were senseless.
So gullible, he crossed acceptance with kindness.
Now too late, she's slowly sucked him limp and lifeless.

Shoulda asked more questions when she was stalking you.
Coulda solved everything if you weren't too lazy to have a clue.
Woulda prevented her from trapping you and doing her voodoo.
Now she's taken the house and kids and all your money, too.

Lilac Bush 95

On Degradation...

I pray that you are well...

Inspired by 3 John 1:2

Grandpa

My grandpa was a drunkard;
That's all of him I've known.
Up the street, he stumbled nightly
From a tavern that he owned.

My grandpa was a drunkard;
From a child observed as such.
We lived in a multifamily he
bought
When others didn't have much.

My grandpa was a drunkard.
His story still untold.
An accomplished man was
covered
But a bachelor's degree did hold.

My grandpa was a drunkard.
He once fixed large boats with
cranes.
An Aleutian Navy veteran,
But he never called me by name.

My grandpa was a drunkard;
A Black man from the South.
High goals achieved, but never
rewarded;
He never opened his mouth.

My grandpa was a drunkard.
My grandma was the cause
Of the pain he took out on her;
Then hid in his room to withdraw.

An uncelebrated life, unrated;
Through time, I've learned about
him.
Hard-working, frustrated,
Broken, and battered; all of this
within.

My grandpa was not a drunkard;
Just an average man with big
dreams.
Against racial tides, he pushed
hard,
To others, his battle, not what it
seemed.

So, grandpa, if you hear me,
Through children, your
achievements live.
Your dreams of succeeding are not
in vain.
To you, accolades we give!

98 Lilac Bush

Figure 40: Grandpa

Lilac Bush 99

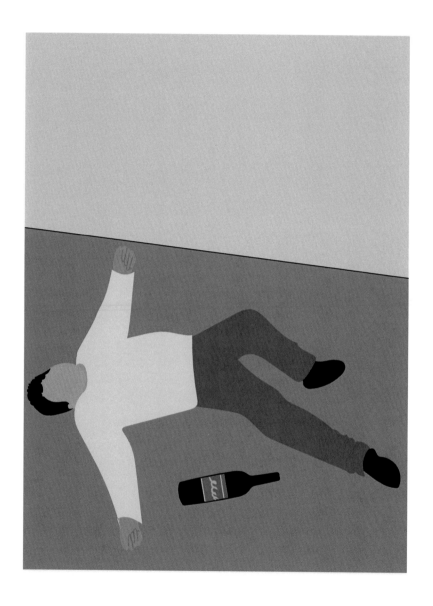

100 Lilac Bush

Figure 41: Foe

Foe

Booze was your friend
When you were lonely;
Played games with your head.

Made you strong
When you were weak;
Left you crooked on the bed.

Made you fly
Instead of walk;
Tossed down in a contorted pose.

Helped you speak
When you were quiet;
Left you with a broken nose.

You said you loved,
But it was stronger;
Forced fingers down your throat.

You could swim
Like an Olympian;
Next, a life ring to stay afloat.

Needed schooling;
It was your teacher;
Now a pocket full of lint.

Picked you up
When you fell down;
But knocked you down again.

Lilac Bush 101

102 Lilac Bush

Figure 42: Nigga

Nigga

"Nigger," we were branded
As if we were herd.
From Mastah it was handed;
And we've carried that word.

Stolen from Africa
Our original birthplace.
Brought to America
And deemed the "Nigger" race.

That word personified
Took on an evil form;
Our humanity denied;
Our dignity torn.

It spit in our face
When we tried to get up.
It kicked out our teeth;
Our pain never enough.

As entertainment fair,
It fed us to dogs.
Left our kids bare
And fed them to hogs.

It herded us like animals;
Hands and feet chained.
Lined up and pulled;
Metal deep ingrained.

Hung on display,
It ripped off our skin.
Forced a new name
And torn from our kin.

It raped our women
As her husband was there.
Left him lost and broken
To comfort her and care.

"Nigga" or "Nigger"
These words are the same.
Using it triggers;
Breathes pain from the grave.

Unbelievable shock
Our ancestors would be in
To hear that word mocked
By our people without feeling.

"Nigga" in songs and rap;
"Nigga" in games played;
"Nigga" to fill in gaps;
Abuse it in every way.

But our ancestors would recognize
Mastah's ideals espoused.
Deep within those people lies
That "Nigga" from the house.

Lilac Bush 103

On Justice...

Let justice flow like the waters and morality like
a raging river.

Inspired by Amos 5:24

Figure 43: Talking to the Corrupt Blue

Talking to the Corrupt Blue

Hey, corrupt blue!
Finally, they see you too!

Hiding under the law;
Targeting our weaknesses and flaws.

Standing on racism systemic;
Woven into our nation's fabric;

Killing our innocent as they run;
Killing our innocent for fun.

At last, the outrage grows!
Because, now, the whole world knows!

We're all on to your game.
You bring shame to our nation's great name.

That badge you wear means virtue.
Only honor true blue pursue.

So, step out of that outfit!
You don't deserve it! You're unfit!

108 Lilac Bush

Figure 44: Blue Monster

Blue Monster

Mom and auntie were screaming
While we were making mud pies.

That blue monster came again.
Now another uncle has died.

Standing in his doorway
In the wrong place at the wrong time.

A familiar game it played.
Every weekend it came for playtime.

Innocent blood on its hands
And dripping from its teeth.

Subjected to the game;
Due to justice, it claimed to seek.

On Foundation...

A house cannot stand, if it's divided.

Inspired by Mark 3:25

Figure 45: Modern Day Polygamy

Modern Day Polygamy

Some people think polygamy is extinct;
Over, abandoned, discontinued, complete.
The topic at hand makes our stomachs sink.
Women controlled by one man reeks.

But this polygamy that we so seek to scorn
Has crept in and taken another form.
It sleeps in her bed, all cozy and warm.
So thoughtful, it cooks her breakfast in the morn.

Enjoys music with her and dances all night;
Shares a loving gaze; its eyes are so bright.
Affectionate and tender, it holds her so tight;
But fangs are so big, in the family, it bites.

Birthed from the system and a product of sin;
Now, from outside, dads observe their children.
The family, this monster, dismantles with a grin.
To her door, on a red carpet, stepped right on in.

Our queens have taken the reigns on the throne.
Failed attempts at love she is prone.
Due to generational curses, with kids, all alone.
Story of abandonment, she continually bemoans.

Our traditional families have been stolen and hijacked.
Ever since slavery, we've been under attack.
Our kids disconnected, with weight on their backs.
They continue to suffer, which is really whack.

Modern-day polygamy, not given too much thought.
Damaged over time, forgetting what we were taught.
Family structure and values, at onetime sought.
Let's get back to our base or continue to rot.

Lilac Bush 113

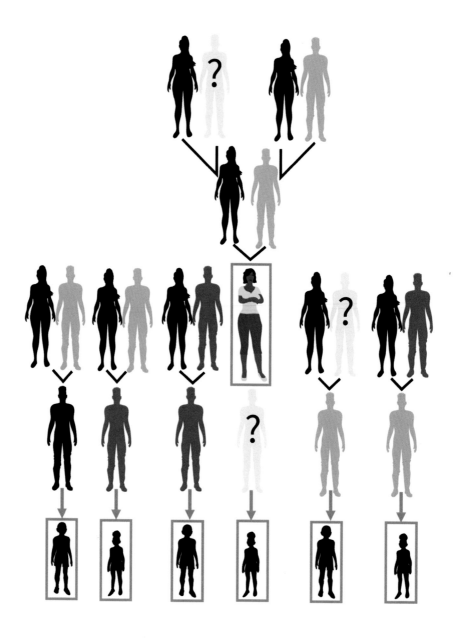

Figure 46: Prevent the Shatter

Prevent the Shatter

When a window of glass is cracked,
Over time, with the drastic changes
Of weather, this crack permeates.
From one end of its surface to the other,
That crack multiplies into more cracks;
And those cracks do the same;
Until the cracks spread across the surface.
While these cracks are multiplying,
Fragments are born.
Once the cracks riddle the entire glass,
It shatters, exploding into small pieces.
Leaving remnants of a generation
Once strong in their beliefs and culture
To wonder generations in,
"What is happening?"

Let's prevent the shatter.

"Uncomfortable" Shell

The truth about racism against us Black Americans is,
It will never end.
But racism doesn't prevent our growth from within.

If we lift that "uncomfortable" shell of racism,
What would outsiders see?

But unsightly happenings of which
Many of us disagree.

Women refuse to close their legs;
Oblivious of their worth.

Pregnancy among our youth
From our music immersed.

Most children are without dads.
Even with force,
Dads won't take their stance.

Our culture consists of whimsical fads;
Men refuse to pull up their pants;

Education is last on the list.
Therefore, poverty is extreme.

Degradation of each other
With Nigga calling and murders;
What does this all mean?!

That "uncomfortable" shell of racial injustice
Has been exactly what we've deemed

Necessary to avoid progress
And remain snug
In a shadow of blame.

So outsiders won't encounter
The true reason for our shame.

Many choosing to stay in place
Due to fears of the unknown.

Conformed to darkness under this shell,
For some, has become home.

Lifting will undoubtedly expose
What we work hard to hide.

Disinterested progress, we make excuses,
In hopes it will magically subside.

Freedom rain comes with
Pounding knocks as a reminder.

Figure 47: "Uncomfortable" Shell

On Love...

God is love and we are created in the image of
God; so let's love.

Inspired by 1 John 4:7

120 Lilac Bush

Figure 48: Our Love

Our Love

Our love was fumbled and slipped through our hands;
Escaped through our fingers like hourglass sand;
Taken for granted and put on a shelf;
To seek in the darkness, but nothing was felt.

It went on a trip but fell off a boat;
Got lost at sea and struggled to float;
Miraculously survived and washed ashore;
Then stolen by pirates, gambled, and squandered.

Toted at a market in burlap, it fell through;
Kicked like a futbol, then a sewer fell into.
Carried by rodents and taken street level;
Then found by someone in awe of its bevels.

Our love, like a jewel, so precious, so rare,
When gawked at its beauty, do nothing but stare.
Our love, personified, died and came back to us;
Supernaturally, it walked out of a cave like Lazarus.

Held in loose grip and fell to the ground,
Our love was once lost, but now again, found.

122 Lilac Bush

Figure 49: Waiting for Your Other

Waiting for Your Other

Waiting for your significant "other"
Can be a daunting task.
But hang on in there, sister or brother;
This loneliness won't last.

Waiting is a virtue;
That standard you can't surpass.
It sets you apart from the rest;
Exhibits value of a higher class.

It shows that you love yourself
And want the best of all.
An "other" customized by God;
That order is not too tall.

Your body is a temple.
It's an honor to treat it as such.
The way you present your body,
Respect returned will be that much.

Don't squander yourself for love,
Or sell yourself short for proof.
It's not about who you can attract.
Affirmation would prove you're loose.

In the meantime, while waiting,
Condition yourself for your "other."
Treat yourself, first, with the best.
Self-love, start to smother.

You'll see. Your love will come knocking
On the door of your beating heart.
You'll both immediately connect.
Then true love with your "other" will start.

Lilac Bush 123

Slow Dance

Intertwined,
Your heart beats with mine.

Standing so close
Our love's an overdose

Of pleasure so high
It brings a tear to my eye.

One hand on your thigh;
The other on your back
As your hands keep track

From my head down my spine
To music as we grind.

Our lips come together.
Our tongues probe with pleasure.

Kissing in circular motion;
Bodies submerged in an ocean

Of feelings we enjoy;
Inhibitions destroyed.

Together we romance
As we oh so slow dance.

Figure 50: Slow Dance

Equal Song

Love is not control.
You've got this thing all wrong.
Love is when two hearts meet,
Respect each other,
And sing an equal song.

Not caging one
And expecting him to sing
With a voice that sounds free, but
not.

Caging him;
Listening by yourself;
Gaining pleasure until his voice rots.

Monitoring his words
And forcing him to sing a song
That you only whistle;

As he cooperates
So your ego won't hurt;
Waiting on dismissal.

Monitoring a situation
You call love;
But you're sadly mistaken.

Love is an agreement
Between two free hearts
Connected and overtaken;

By a mutual love,
Well-wishing,
With trust and respect.

Both willing to
Give their all;
Work hard at and correct.

To enjoy equally,
Real love,
This agreement brings.

To enjoy equally,
The songs, together,
Most beautifully they sing.

126 Lilac Bush

Figure 51: Equal Song

128 Lilac Bush

Figure 52: When We Met

When We Met

Before we met, God showed me you were on your way.
We embraced, but I couldn't see your face that day.
I made the announcement to everyone in my family.
They brushed it off and chose not to believe me.

I started visualizing and planning my wedding;
Drawing the details of the dress on my bedding.
One month later, in a suit, with a bow tie and suspenders,
You showed up at my door, and I knew God was your sender.

Picked up for a Christening with mutual friends,
You were the driver, so your car I sat in.
When you looked through the rearview, my heart did a
plummet.
Felt slightly strange, my heart in my stomach.

The connection not made yet; we had fun that day;
We laughed and talked so much; the time got away.
After that, our relationship took off and took flight.
We talked on the phone all day and all night.

Fast forward to today; four kids later.
Loving you through the years; nothing's been greater.
Through ups and downs in our marriage so deep,
I thank God for you when I hold you while I sleep.

You're my hero, my confidant, my lover, and my friend.
This journey of ours, will never end.
God paired us together, and we stuck like glue.
Loving, caring, handsome, faithful, unmistakable you!

On Friends...

Choose your friends cautiously.

Inspired by Proverbs 12:26

Good Friend

Let me tell you about your "good friend."
This may be hard for you to hear.
But listen closely, she wants your man,
Tell that "friend" to disappear!

Have you noticed she's always around?
And digs for every detail?
You keep complaining and putting him down
While she's heavy on your trail.

Steady sucking up all your dirt
And using it to suit herself.
You have no idea, but she wants your man.
Keep your business to yourself!

You're attractive, intelligent, and focused.
You have everything she wants.
So, to prove that you're not better than her,
Your man, with sex, she taunts.

She's always available to help you out;
Even picks your kids up from school.
At your house on your way from work;
Doesn't she have something else to do?!

Always stuck under you and your man;
Now you both on her depend.
She even massages that crook in his back.
Oh, yeah! She's a real "good friend!"

And that man you're with, put him in check.
He fueled her with a bit of flirtation.
Get rid of him, or he'd better come correct!
Now she swears she's in a competition.

So, girl, hear me out, it'll be alright;
Befriending her was a huge mistake.
Get rid of that so-called "good friend."
She's nothing but a slithering snake!

Figure 53: Good Friend

On God...

Their is love and protection in the presence of Almighty God.

Inspired by Psalm 91

136 Lilac Bush

Figure 54: Lilac Bush

Lilac Bush

Wondrously nurturing, the lilac bush grew.
Mesmerizing fragrance, all around us she blew.
Loving and caring, large family drawn near;
In awe of her beauty, all stopped, gazed, and stared.

A symbol of love to those all around;
A home in her presence would always be found.
Her offspring of flowers, faithfully devoted;
Proud of each one, softly she doted.

Raised by God with sunlight and water;
Resilient endurance; weather, colder or hotter;
Up from the ground and tended by God;
Pruned by angels from Heaven above.

Like an elixir, our ailments she cured.
Time in her presence, you'd hunger for more.
Intolerable summer days, with hot sun aglow,
Her branches hovered and provided shadow.

Our house burned down, and to our dismay,
Torn from our chests, she was taken away.
Taken by God, our hearts could not bear
This loss of life, so precious, so rare.

My grandmother thoughtfully planted
    this bush.
Through generations raised, one
    dreadful night took
The love of our lives, such pain
    we mourned and cried.
Our bush turned to embers
    the night grandma died.

Lilac Bush 137

One Easter Sunday

Found God at church one Easter Sunday when I was eleven.
Everyone was happy. That day, I found out there's a Heaven.
First time at church, my hair curled; mom dressed me so nice.
That was the beginning of my love for Jesus Christ.

The missionaries sat me down and told me I had sin.
I didn't know that was possible since there's nowhere I'd ever been.
It was my first time at church, so I was a bit out of touch.
But on that Easter Sunday, I learned so much!

Jesus loved me with such depth; He died on a cross.
And without this sacrifice, my soul would be lost.
As I looked around, I saw happiness like never before.
Young people praising God and the Spirit outpoured.

The music was so powerful as the choir sang with praise.
The organ and tambourines set my soul ablaze.
The preacher spoke of God's love and grace from the Word.
They taught me of God's Son, something I'd never heard.

That day marked the start of a journey with Jesus as my friend.
Although, that day, I had no idea God knew I needed Him.
Through good times and bad, this love, I could never live without.
And every day since then, I've felt His presence throughout.

Figure 55: One Easter Sunday

140 Lilac Bush

Figure 56: Whiter Than Snow

Whiter Than Snow

You blot out my transgressions and sins.
Whiter than snow, You wash me again.
Over and over, I fall from Your grace;
Done some things to hide from Your face.

My maze, I repeatedly find myself in.
Whiter than snow, You wash me again.
Riding through this familiar passage,
Your love rescues me from my wreckage.

You faithfully pull me out of my den.
Whiter than snow, You wash me again.
With eyes on You, I feel anew.
All owed to You; I make my debut.

From darkness, You pull me into Your light!
You give me the strength to continually fight!
Against the enemy, a battle I'll incite!
Great is Your strength and powerful might!

Whiter than snow, You wash me again.

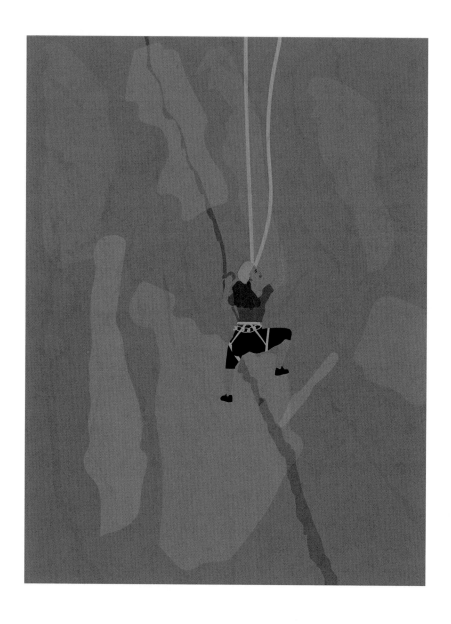

142 Lilac Bush

Figure 57: God is Greater

God is Greater

Exceedingly, abundantly, beyond what we think or imagine;
Splendid is His virtue and righteousness when we examine;

More meaningful than the songs we so passionately sing;
Greater than the sorrow this life occasionally brings;

Higher than the highest mountains we are tasked to climb;
More breathtaking than a picturesque landscape sublime;

Wider than the oceans that stretch across the earth;
Way more profitable than jewels or monetary worth;

Lighter than the burdens we are sometimes required to bear;
Infinite is His mercy, grace, love, and care;

To God, nothing and no one compares.

Figure 58: Rescue

Rescue

In the middle of this storm,
In this ocean of pain,
My body beat hard,
Can't breathe from this rain.

Alone in these waters,
Gave in to my fears,
My eyes were off You
When this storm came severe.

"Lord, do you see me?!"
I once again cry.
But there You were standing
On the waves nearby.

My rescuer! My Savior!
Pull me out from this sadness!
My hope! My strength! My all!
Pull me out from this madness!

With strength so courageous,
You pulled me out of fear.
You pulled me out from that raging storm
And made it disappear.

Now, my joy is overwhelming!
My hope is now restored!
You've rescued me once again;
And carried me back to shore.

146 Lilac Bush

Figure 59: Never Alone

Never Alone

An abandoned jar
Someone left standing
Alone and forgotten.

It's dirt-encrusted;
Meant to preserve
And have some function.

Stands by itself;
Metal is rusted,
Against the porch wall.

Through seasons,
It sits waiting
On each rainfall.

Never kicked or disturbed,
Just sitting alone
And tarrying;

For someone to
Rescue, wash it,
Or carry it.

But God sends the rain
To love it
With overflow.

More joy than
The pampered jars
Could ever know.

His rain has come
At times
It felt disowned.

Welcomed taps of drops
Remind this jar
It's never alone.

Lilac Bush 147

Figure 60: A River's Work

A River's Work

As the River of water flows courageously upstream,
Tongues of glory to God with praises it sings.
Dancing in rhythm as it caresses the ground;
Along with all creatures making wonderful sounds.

Gathered with rocks and boulders through mountains;
Springs up from the earth like a never-ending fountain;
Gives life to those who are thirsty and drink;
Embraces all creation who immerse and sink.

It travels upstream and wrangles up all.
Catches and supports those who trust it and fall;
Fills up the well that never runs dry;
And washes away tears of those who cry.

Those who believe, go down and emerge clean.
Baptized to life, born from sin, they gleam.
Duties of God, this diligent River celebrates.
Congregating with all creation it loves and appreciates.

Worship in agreement with those all around;
With beauty and glorious purpose, it sounds.
Like a trumpet, crashes through life on its course;
Proudly committed to performing God's works.

Into His Fold

Do you know God?
He's standing right there.
His arms are wide open;
No reason to fear.

He knew you before
Your mom and dad were born.
He welcomes you home.
Is there a reason you're torn?

His love is perfection;
Strength when you're weak.
He comes to your rescue
When situations look bleak.

To win your love
Is His ultimate goal.
His hand is extended
To pull you into His fold.

Figure 61: Into His Fold

Lilac Bush 151

A Mother's Prayer

On the shoulders of her mom,
She fervently prayed.
Now on my mom's shoulders,
I'm before You today.

I pray for my children
And generations to come.
That before them, that battle,
They've already won.

That mountain that's stubborn
And refuses to move,
Will be pushed out their way
And they'll walk right on through.

Those demons that surround them
Will frightfully flee,
And be cast to the midst
And depths of the sea.

They'll learn to trust You
And cling to Your Word.
And through it, their prayers
Are already heard.

In confidence, they'll walk
With Your soldiers behind.
Fighting for their triumph;
Only victories they'll find!

Prosperity will find them
With favor and merit.
Wealth for generations,
Their children will inherit.

My God, please surround them
With your love and protection.
Cover them with Your blood
That flows with perfection.

Their children, and children's
children
Will surely be blessed.
In the clothes of Your Royalty,
They'll proudly be dressed.

God, in my children, spring up
And do a new thing.
My heart will forever praise You.
To Your glory, I'll sing!

152 Lilac Bush

Figure 62: A Mother's Prayer

154 Lilac Bush

Figure 63: God Loves You

God Loves You

Before your mom and dad were born,
Before you were conceived or formed,
God knew your name.

He knows every hair in your mane.
Broken, yet, He still loves you the same.
God's love does not change.

His love does not falter or range.
His love is never estranged.
God's love has no bounds.

No greater friend can be found.
His love is peaceful and sound.
God loves you!

Please Heal This Woman of God
(A Prayer)

God, You're greater than any sickness or infirmity.
You're greater than any doubt that causes uncertainty.

Your miraculous hand touches from head to toe.
Your wonder-working power is capable, I know.

With faith in Your abilities, I'm asking You to heal;
This woman of God, who believes and knows You're so real.

Surround her with Your angels and lovingly care.
Reassure her of Your presence because I can't be there.

I trust in Your strength, this sickness You will cure;
And praise You in advance; you're my God and Savior!

Figure 64: Please Heal This Woman of God   Lilac Bush 157

On Breakthrough...

Anything is possible with God on your side.

Inspired by Luke 1:37

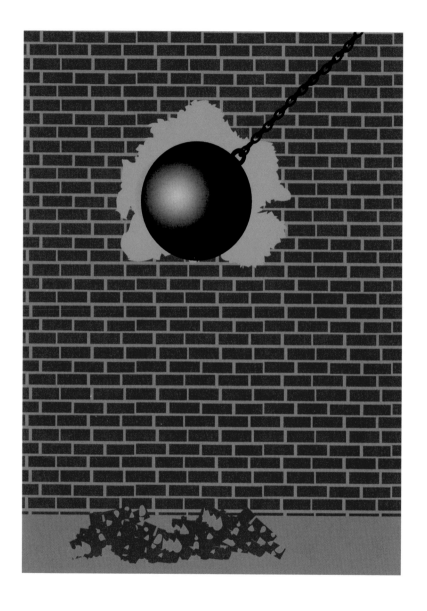

160 Lilac Bush

Figure 65: Guilt

Guilt

Guilt is a tall wall
Built with bricks of shame.
It serves as a barricade
Preventing progress.
Break down this wall
With the strength
That God gives.
His force is like
The ball on
A demolition crane.
It will obliterate
That tall wall to dust.

Figure 66: Go Get It

Go Get It

So, you're working in a job that pays minimum wage;
Struggling to pay bills since you were legal age;
Working extremely hard from shift to shift;
Breaking your back just to buy yourself a gift.

To advance in your career, not given too much thought.
Education is not for you, so nothing was further sought.
Like a hamster around the wheel, with all of your might,
You're so content with this hustle of everyday life.

Why are you content with settling for less?
Use your brain, instead of running mindless.
Four years out of life is not too much time.
You just spent four years boxed in like a mime.

Now proceed to convince yourself that you need the money.
But in just four years, you can cross the line from poverty.
Just getting by in this life, is it really worth it?
A sacrifice for a pinch of time means more money in your
pocket.

Pick yourself up, dust yourself off and start all over again.
Go at it like a raging bull and finish to the end.
Forget about how outrageous it sounds and go get your degree.
Your life will be much better off. Just you wait and see.

Imagination

Imagination can take you
To places you've never been.
A vehicle to get away
And make a lot of friends.

Break from this confining space;
In your mind, you can transcend.
Anything you desire to be;
Just indulge and make pretend.

Step out in a star-studded gown;
"Excuse me, are you talking to me?"
On white sand, relaxing, getting some sun
Under a coconut tree.

You're in control, so give it a go.
The places are endless, you'll see.
Let your mind drift and float on a trip
To places you want to be.

Figure 67: Imagination

Figure 68: Boxed

Boxed

Are you satisfied in that box you're sitting in;
Fully enclosed with six walls on your skin;
Happy and content all snug and warm;
Sitting cross-legged until slightly deformed?
Comfy in your box with that grimaced forced grin.

So much space in your box to do stuff like spin;
Talk through those walls to all your boxed friends;
Jump up and down and pounce on the ground;
Shuffle around until you're upside down;
Just fine in your box, staying busy within.

No sun in that box. Its lighting's quite dim
So, you joke to yourself instead of feeling grim.
You make your box roll to the left and the right;
Hang your head slight to sleep through the night;
Just making it work in your cozy, quaint bin.

No judgment at all; just wondering why;
With God-given gifts therein you lie?
All that's inside, you hide from the world.
Break out that box and give it a whirl!
Tear down those walls and give it a try!

The sun will shine down with a welcoming embrace.
The grass will catch you as you dance to celebrate.
Gracefully, the wind will join you this day.
Unboxed friends will see you on your way.
Break out from that box! Make the world your space!

Acknowledgments

First, I thank God for the opportunity to share these poems! With God, all things are possible. And I am honored that He chose me to convey these crucial messages to the world!

I thank my husband, Paul, and our adult children, Paul, Jr., Ikenna, Tobechi, and Christina, for their patience, love, support, insight, contributions, and opinions.

Thanks to my extended family. My love for you shines through in these reminiscent poems focused on our childhood. Also, you gave me lots of love and encouragement as my alpha readers.

Finally, thanks to all editors and beta readers for your insight and eye for detail throughout this writing process.

Sincerely,

Pamela C. Nwokeji
Author of Lilac Bush

Bibliography

[1] Children in single-parent families by race in the United States. (2020, December). KIDS COUNT data center: A project of the Annie E. Casey Foundation. https://datacenter.kidscount.org/ data/bar/107-children-in-single-parent-families-by-race#1/any/fal se/1729/10,11,9,12,1,185,13/431.

[2] Kremer, John. (2020, July 3). The Tragedy of Children from Single-Parent Homes . . . Medium. https://medium.com/ commentary-for-today/the-sadness-of-children-from-single-parent-homes-1cf00358474e.

[3] Who lives in Poverty USA? (2021). Poverty USA. https://www. povertyusa.org/facts.

[4] Childhood Sexual Abuse. (2021). AAMFT. https://www.aamft. org/Consumer_Updates/Childhood_Sexual_Abuse.aspx.

[5] Johnson, James W. "Lift Ev'ry Voice and Sing." (1900). Learning For Justice. (2021). https://www.learningforjustice.org/ classroom-resources/texts/lift-every-voice-and-sing#:~:text=This%20 text%20is%20in%20the%20public%20domain.%20 %E2%80%9CLift,believe%20it%20reflects%20an%20aspect%20 of%20African-American%20history.
Text in the Public Domain.

[6] Johnson, James Weldon. Johnson, J. Rosamond. "Lift Ev'ry Voice and Sing." (1900). The World Tomorrow. (June 1929). https:// onlineexhibits.library.yale.edu/s/lift-every-voice/media/7788.
Text in the Public Domain.